Rock Stars

CRYSTALS AND GEMSTONES

Chris and Helen Pellant

Copyright © ticktock Entertainment Ltd 2008
First published in Great Britain in 2008 by ticktock Media Ltd,
2 Orchard Business Centre, North Farm Road, Tunbridge Wells, Kent, TN2 3XF

ticktock project editor: Julia Adams
ticktock project designer: Emma Randall
ticktock picture researcher: Lizzie Knowles
series consultant: Terry Jennings

We would like to thank: Graham Rich, Joe Harris

ISBN-13: 978 1 84696 696 5 pbk

Printed in China

Picture credits (t=top; b=bottom; c=centre; l=left; r=right):
age fotostock/ SuperStock: 3l, 21tr. iStock: 3E, 5t, 9t, 10cl, 12tl, 12cr x2, 12cl, 13cr, 22t, 23tr, 23cl. Ben
Mangor/ SuperStock: 15t. North Wind Picture Archives/ Alamy: 14b. Jack Novak/ SuperStock: 23bl.
Chris & Helen Pellant: 3B, 6t, 6c, 6b, 7t, 8bl x2, 9c, 9b, 11tr, 16 all, 17l x3, 18 all, 19l x3, 20 all, 21l x3.
Photodisc/ Photolibrary: 7br. Photolibrary Group: OFC c. Pool Photograph/ Corbis: 22c. Scientifica/
Visuals Unlimited/ Alamy: 11r. Shutterstock: OFC background, OFC t x3, 1, 2, 3A, C, D, F, G, H, J, K, L, 4tl,
4bl, 4br, 5bl, 5bc, 5br, 7c, 7bl, 8tl, 10tl, 10cr, 10bl, 10br, 11l x3, 12bl x2, 12br, 13tl, 13tr, 13cl, 13bl, 13br, 14tl,
14cl, 14cr, 15c all, 17tr, 17br x2, 19tr, 19br, 21br x2, 23tl, 25tl, OBC. Javier Trueba/ MSF/ Science Photo
Library: 22ft. Roland Weihrauch/ dpa/ Corbis: 22b. Wikipedia: 23cr.

Contents

Words that appear in **bold** are explained in the glossary.

What Are Crystals?

Crystals are shiny, solid materials. They can have many different shapes, sizes and colours. Crystals have many flat surfaces and straight edges.

Crystals are found in many places on Earth. Some form in caves deep underground. Others form inside stones or by the seaside.

Crystals can be very bright and colourful. These are quartz crystals.

Sometimes, crystals are shiny and metallic, like this pyrite.

It's a Fact!
Naturally formed ice is a kind of crystal, too. But the ice that forms in your freezer isn't. It forms too quickly to form a crystal structure.

Icicles on a branch

Crystals are all around you. Foods like salt and sugar are made of many tiny crystals. We even have crystals in our bodies. Our bones are made of millions of very small crystals.

We also use crystals to make things, like clocks and even game consoles! Sometimes we shape them in beautiful ways. Then they are called gemstones. We use gemstones in jewellery.

ow Do Crystals Form?

All rocks are made of at least one **mineral**. Sometimes minerals grow into hard, shiny objects with flat surfaces. These kinds of minerals are called crystals.

Crystals in rocks

Most of the Earth's crystals were formed millions of years ago. Crystals form when **molten rock** from inside the Earth cools and hardens. If the molten rock cools quickly, the crystals in it are tiny. If the rock cools slowly, the crystals can be quite large. Rock that forms in this way is called **igneous rock**.

Granite is an igneous rock.

Sandstone is a sedimentary rock.

Rocks can be worn down by wind, very hot or cold weather, and moving ice or water. The rocks break down into tiny grains called sediment. This sediment can have tiny pieces of crystal in it. Sometimes sediment forms layers. The bottom layers get squashed deep underground by the top ones. Then the bottom layers form **sedimentary rock**.

Gneiss is a metamorphic rock.

Deep under the Earth's surface there is a lot of heat and pressure. This can change igneous and sedimentary rocks into **metamorphic rock**. When the rocks get changed, the crystals in them change, too. You can see this when granite has been changed into gneiss: granite looks speckled, but gneiss looks stripey.

Surface crystals

A lot of crystals form on the surface of the Earth, too. This can happen in many different ways.

Water that cools down naturally slowly turns into ice crystals.

Sometimes molten rock bursts to the surface through a volcano. Then it cools down and forms crystals.

When seawater evaporates, salt crystals form.

Crystal Shapes

Crystals can form in many different shapes. They can have many surfaces or just a few. The surfaces can be different shapes and joined in different ways, too.

The surfaces of crystals are called faces. When the faces of a crystal join together, they can make a shape that looks the same from all sides. These crystals are symmetrical.

This is pyrite. It has six square **>>** faces. They form **cube**-shaped crystals. They look like dice!

Natural rock base

<< This is a fluorite crystal. It is made of eight faces. The faces all have the shape of a triangle. The crystal looks like two pyramids stuck together!

This is mica. It is >>
one of the crystals
that forms the rock
granite. Mica forms
in very flat,
thin crystals.

It's a Fact!

Crystals that have
symmetrical shapes are
also called 'perfect
crystals'.

Gypsum crystals >>
are very thin and
long. They look a
bit like needles.

This is haematite. >>
It has a bubbly
shape. The bubbles
are formed by tiny
crystals. They are so
small, you cannot
see them with the
naked eye.

Which Crystal?

There are many different ways of finding out the type of a crystal. As well as its shape, you can look at its colour and you can even test its hardness.

Colourful crystals

Crystals come in many different shades and colours. Sometimes, they even have more than one colour! You can sometimes work out the type of a crystal by its colour.

Rose quartz gets its name from its colour. It is always a very light pink.

Citrine is a combination of white and brilliant yellow. It is often formed into gemstones and used for jewellery.

Topaz usually has a soft golden colour. When it has a hint of pink, it is called imperial topaz.

Malachite is a very intense green. This is why it used to be used to make paint.

You can use the Crystal Collector section to find out more about the different colours of crystals.

Crystal hardness

We use a scale to test the hardness of crystals. It runs from 1 to 10. Crystals that have a measurement of 10 are the hardest. The crystals that are higher up on the scale can scratch the ones lower down on the scale.

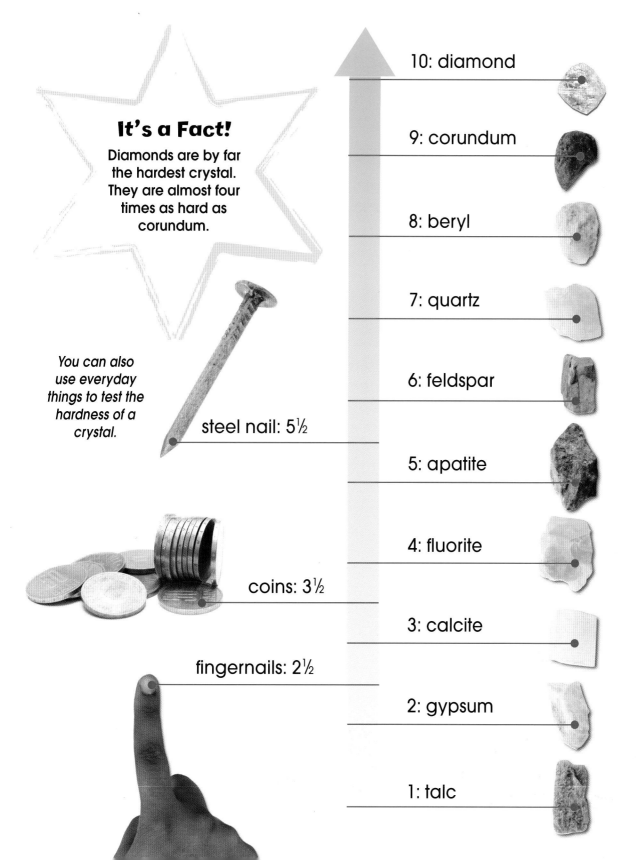

It's a Fact!
Diamonds are by far the hardest crystal. They are almost four times as hard as corundum.

You can also use everyday things to test the hardness of a crystal.

steel nail: 5½

coins: 3½

fingernails: 2½

10: diamond

9: corundum

8: beryl

7: quartz

6: feldspar

5: apatite

4: fluorite

3: calcite

2: gypsum

1: talc

What Are Gemstones?

A gemstone is a mineral or crystal that has been cut and polished. It may be a sparkling diamond, or shiny emerald. Gemstones are often very expensive.

From crystal to gemstone

When crystals are turned into gemstones, they are cut and polished in a special way to make them shine and sparkle. A lot of gemstones are made from crystals that are very rare. This is why gemstones are also called precious stones.

Orpiment is cut and polished to make rubies.

Cut and polished corundum is called sapphire.

Beryl is cut and polished into emerald.

Organic gemstones

Some gemstones are made of materials from animals or plants. This is why they are called **organic** gemstones. Unlike crystals, they cannot be tested for hardness.

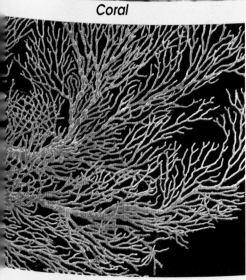

Resin

Amber

Amber

Amber is made of tree **resin**. When the resin seeps out of the bark of trees, it slowly hardens. If it hardens over millions of years, it turns into amber.

Coral

Coral beads

Coral

Coral is a very hard material that is sometimes formed in tree-like shapes. It is made by millions of tiny creatures that live in tropical oceans.

Pearl necklace

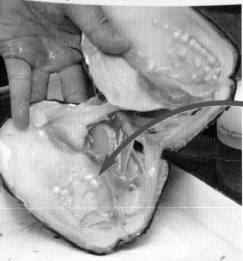

Oyster with pearls

Pearl

Sometimes sand grains can get trapped inside the shell of a shellfish, such as an oyster. The animal inside the shell starts to coat the grain of sand with very small shiny white crystals. Eventually, this turns the sand grain into a pearl!

ow We Use Gemstones

For centuries, gemstones have been very important in many cultures. They can be a sign power and wealth. Some people believe certain gemstones bring good luck, too.

Healing powers

Ancient Egyptians believed that coloured gemstones could heal people. Today, some people still practise this type of healing. They believe that placing crystals and gemstones on the body will help cure illnesses.

Good hunting

Native American tribes have been crafting objects made of turquoise since 1000 BCE. The gemstone is used in jewellery and has a special meaning for each tribe. The Pueblo believe that attaching a piece of turquoise to a gun or bow will give them perfect aim.

A Pueblo tribesman

Royal gems

Diamonds are the hardest and most precious gemstones. For centuries they have been a symbol of wealth. Diamonds are often used on royal crowns and precious jewellery.

*Topaz
November*

*Turquoise
December*

*Garnet
January*

*Amethyst
February*

*Aquamarine
March*

*Opal
October*

Birthstones

Many countries have a tradition of birthstones. These are gemstones that each represent a month of the year. Many people wear the gemstone of the month they were born in. What is your birthstone?

*Diamond
April*

*Sapphire
September*

*Peridot
August*

*Ruby
July*

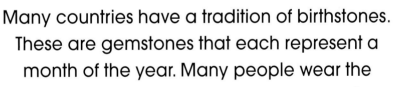

*Pearl
June*

*Emerald
May*

Crystal Collector

Common crystals

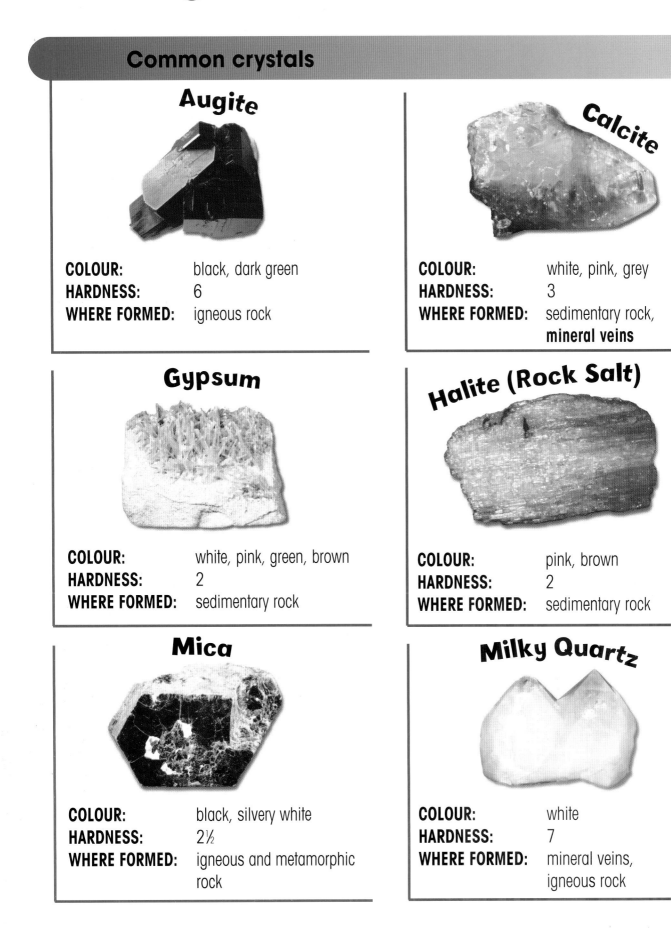

Augite

COLOUR:	black, dark green
HARDNESS:	6
WHERE FORMED:	igneous rock

Calcite

COLOUR:	white, pink, grey
HARDNESS:	3
WHERE FORMED:	sedimentary rock, **mineral veins**

Gypsum

COLOUR:	white, pink, green, brown
HARDNESS:	2
WHERE FORMED:	sedimentary rock

Halite (Rock Salt)

COLOUR:	pink, brown
HARDNESS:	2
WHERE FORMED:	sedimentary rock

Mica

COLOUR:	black, silvery white
HARDNESS:	2½
WHERE FORMED:	igneous and metamorphic rock

Milky Quartz

COLOUR:	white
HARDNESS:	7
WHERE FORMED:	mineral veins, igneous rock

Feldspar

COLOUR: white, pink, bluish
HARDNESS: 6
WHERE FORMED: igneous and metamorphic rock

Hornblende

COLOUR: black, dark green
HARDNESS: 6
WHERE FORMED: igneous rock

Tourmaline

COLOUR: green, pink, black, blue
HARDNESS: 7½
WHERE FORMED: igneous rock

Finding Crystals

You can find crystals in many places. Some rocks are made of crystals. Sometimes, crystals grow inside hollow rocks, too. When you go looking for crystals, it is best to take a few useful things with you:

- A strong rucksack for your finds and other equipment.

- Newspaper or bubble wrap to protect **specimens**.

- A geological hammer for breaking up loose rocks. Always ask an adult to help you with this.

- Goggles to wear when using your hammer.

- A magnifying glass.

- A notebook and pen to record your findings.

Crystal Collector

Gemstones

Aquamarine

COLOUR: pale blue
HARDNESS: 8
WHERE FORMED: igneous rock

Benitoite

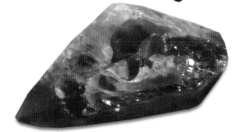

COLOUR: blue
HARDNESS: 6½
WHERE FORMED: metamorphic rock

Citrine

COLOUR: yellow, orange-brown
HARDNESS: 7
WHERE FORMED: mineral veins

Diamond

COLOUR: clear
HARDNESS: 10
WHERE FORMED: volcanic rock

Kunzite

COLOUR: pink
HARDNESS: 7½
WHERE FORMED: igneous rock

Spinel

COLOUR: red, green, blue, black
HARDNESS: 8
WHERE FORMED: metamorphic and
igneous rock

Collecting Gemstones

Cairngorm

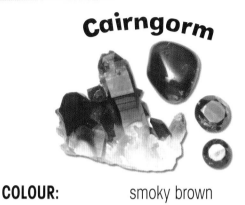

COLOUR:	smoky brown
HARDNESS:	7
WHERE FORMED:	mineral veins, igneous rock

Emerald

COLOUR:	green
HARDNESS:	8
WHERE FORMED:	igneous rock

Zircon

COLOUR:	green
HARDNESS:	8
WHERE FORMED:	igneous rock

 You can easily start a gemstone collection without spending a lot of money. Here are some tips to help you get started:

- Have a look around your town to find out where the nearest gem shop is. You will be able to buy gems at low prices here. They can also give you some great advice on collecting gemstones.

- Mineral dealers sell crystals and gemstones. They have websites, too. If you get in touch with them, they can send you catalogues.

- Join a local mineralogists or gemmologists club. This way you will get to know other collectors. They can also give you lots of advice.

- Visit mineral shows and fairs.

Crystal Collector

More gemstones

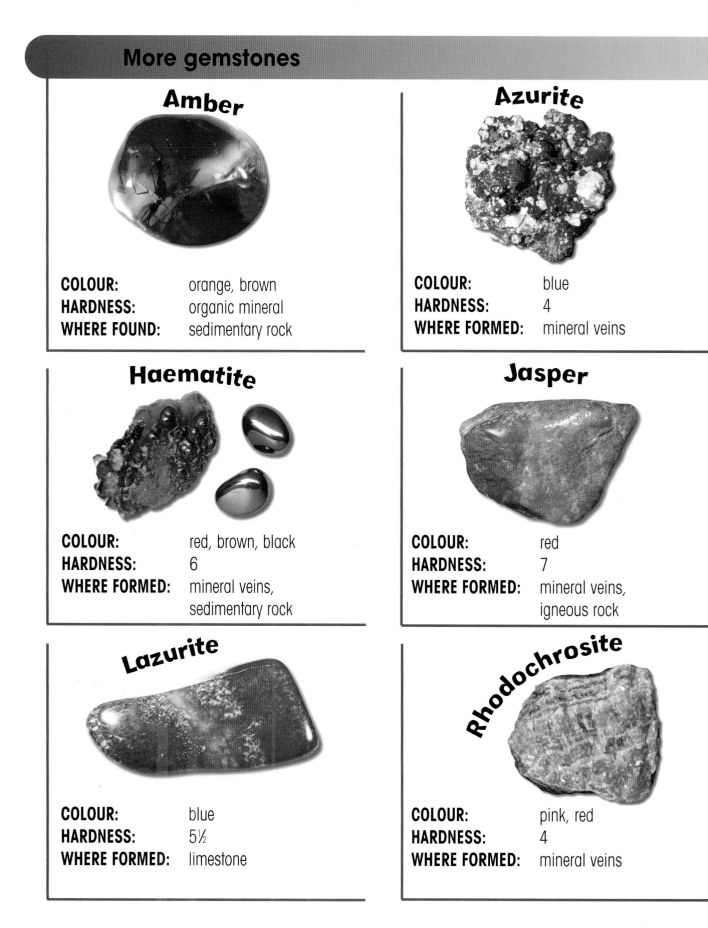

Amber

COLOUR:	orange, brown
HARDNESS:	organic mineral
WHERE FOUND:	sedimentary rock

Azurite

COLOUR:	blue
HARDNESS:	4
WHERE FORMED:	mineral veins

Haematite

COLOUR:	red, brown, black
HARDNESS:	6
WHERE FORMED:	mineral veins, sedimentary rock

Jasper

COLOUR:	red
HARDNESS:	7
WHERE FORMED:	mineral veins, igneous rock

Lazurite

COLOUR:	blue
HARDNESS:	5½
WHERE FORMED:	limestone

Rhodochrosite

COLOUR:	pink, red
HARDNESS:	4
WHERE FORMED:	mineral veins

Your Display

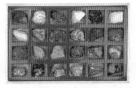

Crystals and gemstones are ideal for display. They are very delicate, so you should keep them away from dust and liquids. The less your crystals are handled the better.

Here are some more hints for displaying crystals and gemstones:

- Make card trays for your specimens, with a name card in the base.

- Put your most showy specimens on display, but preferably behind glass.

- Specimens should be cleaned very carefully with a soft paint brush.

- Leave crystals on their natural rock base to prevent damaging them.

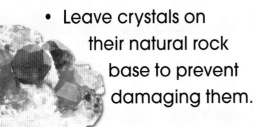

Blue John

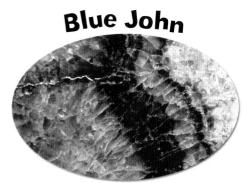

COLOUR:	bands of blue and white
HARDNESS:	4
WHERE FORMED:	veins in limestone

Jet

COLOUR:	black
HARDNESS:	organic mineral
WHERE FOUND:	sedimentary rock

Turquoise

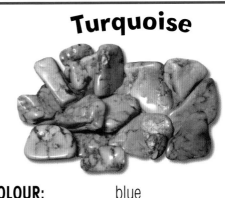

COLOUR:	blue
HARDNESS:	5
WHERE FORMED:	sedimentary and igneous rock

Record Breakers

Biggest crystals

To date, the largest crystals on Earth have been found in northern Mexico. They are made of gypsum and they are around 11 metres long!

Rarest crystal

One of the rarest crystals on Earth is the diamond. Most diamonds are buried deep under the Earth's surface. About 1,000 tonnes of rock need to be moved to get 0.2 grams of diamond!

Oldest large cut diamond

The oldest cut diamond is believed to be the Koh-i-noor ('mountain of light'). It was probably found in India, and was presented to Queen Victoria of England in 1820. Today, it is part of the Crown Jewels.

Gem 'world wonder'

The Amber Room was built in 1711 for the king of Prussia. It was made of over six tonnes of amber and took ten years to build. The Amber Room was destroyed in the Second World War, but rebuilt and completed in 2003. It is in the Catherine Palace in St. Petersburg, Russia.

Did You Know?

Quartz is one of the most common crystals on Earth. There are 16 main types of quartz. They have colours ranging from clear to black!

Rubies were a symbol of power in the Middle Ages. Sometimes, ladies gave rubies to their knights as a sign of love.

Tiny pieces of sharpened diamonds are used as knife blades in operations. This is because they cut very precisely.

Some gems get cut in such a way, that light reflecting off them makes them look like cat eyes.

Quartz crystals are used in many electrical things. They are even used in the chips of credit cards!

The Hope Diamond is a very precious large blue diamond. People believe that whoever owns it will be cursed! It is kept in the Smithsonian Institute, USA.

For thousands of years, people all over the world have tried to tell the future using crystal balls. Usually, these crystal balls are made of quartz.

The weight of gemstones is measured in karats. One karat is 0.2 grams. The higher the karat, the more valuable it is.

Pearls can come in many different colours. Some pearls are even black!

Glossary

Cube Solid shape, like a dice, with six square sides.

Evaporate When something liquid turns into a gas. Water evaporates when it turns into water vapour or steam.

Igneous rock A type of rock formed from the hot molten rock deep underground. When the molten rock bursts to the Earth's surface, it can form igneous rock there, too.

Metamorphic rock A type of rock that has been changed from what it was at first. These changes are caused by heat or pressure deep underground.

Minerals The chemicals that rocks are made of. Many minerals form as crystals.

Mineral veins Masses of minerals that form in cracks in rocks or between rock layers.

Molten rock Extremely hot rock that flows like a liquid.

Organic Anything that lives: plants, animals and humans are all organic.

Resin A thick, sticky material. It is made by many plants like fir or pine trees.

Sedimentary rock A type of rock that is formed as layers of sand or rock grains. The layers form on the sea bed and get pressed together to form solid rocks.

Specimen A piece of a mineral or rock. It can be used as a sample in a collection.

Volcano A hole in the Earth's crust where molten rock bursts to the surface.

Index